EURO STYLE!

Photographic essay by Peter Steiner

First Edition

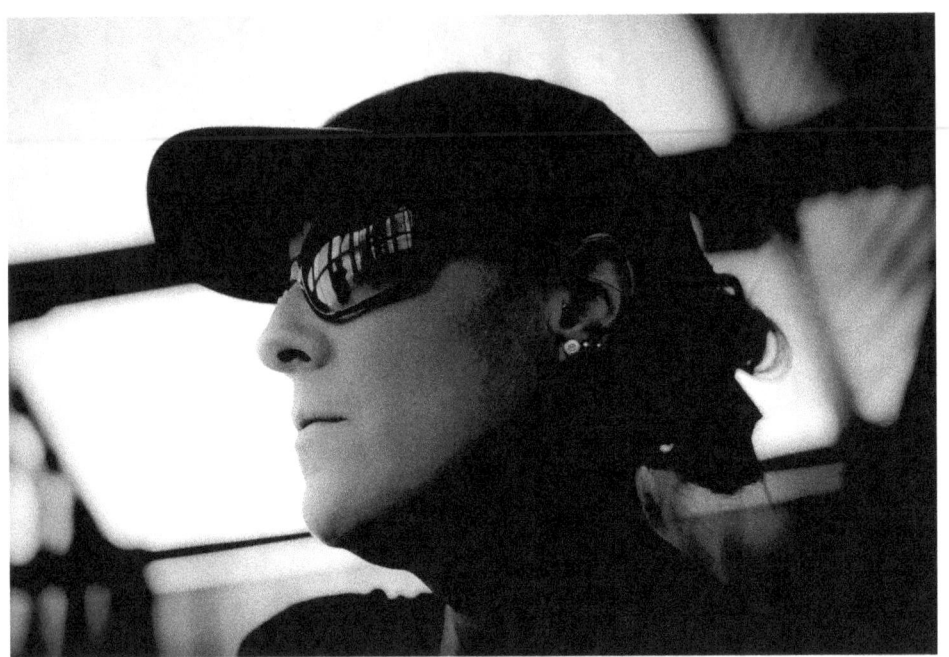

This book is dedicated to my muse and one true love.

She comes in colors ev'rywhere;
She combs her hair
She's like a rainbow
Coming, colors in the air

» Mick Jagger

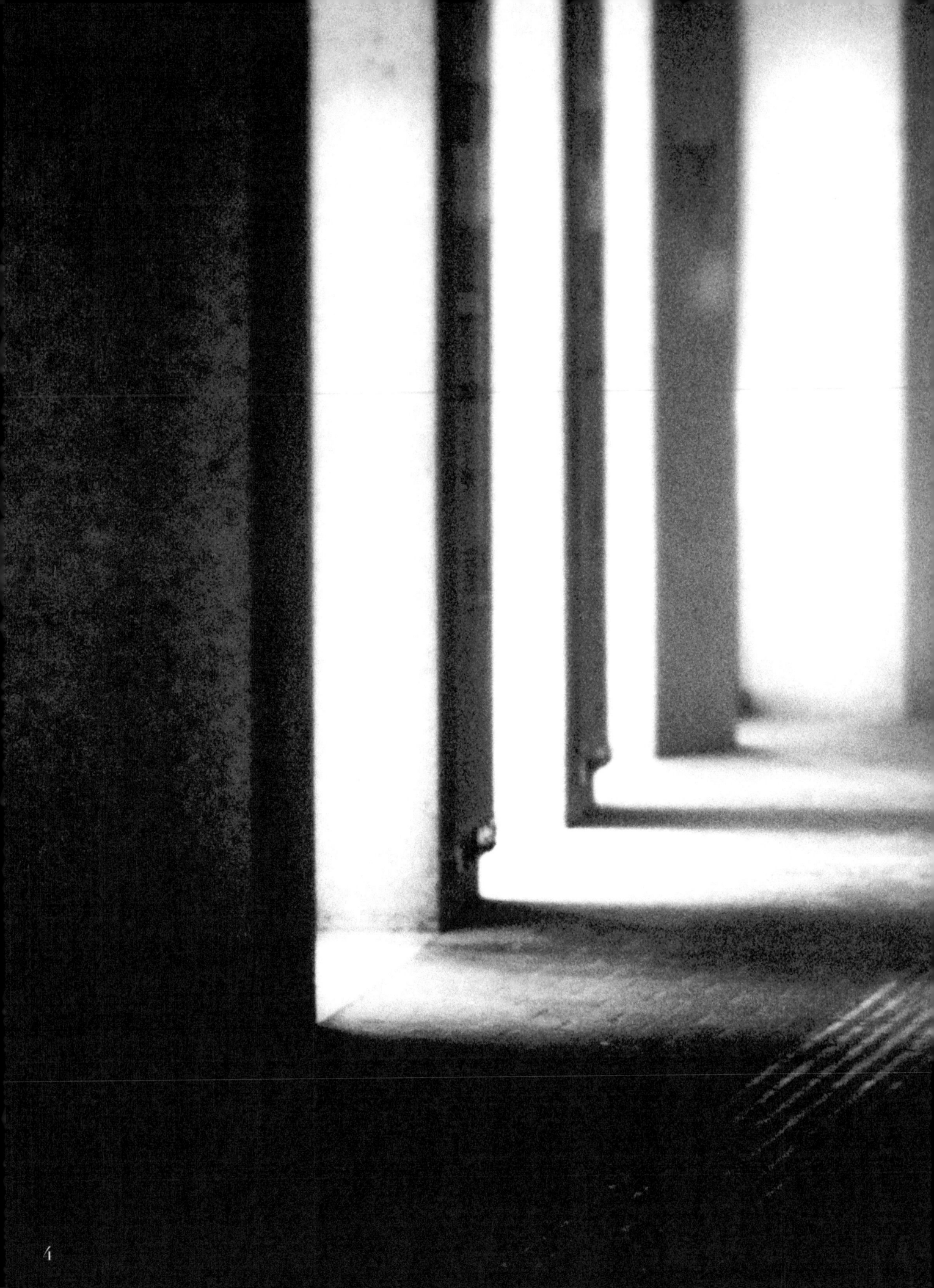

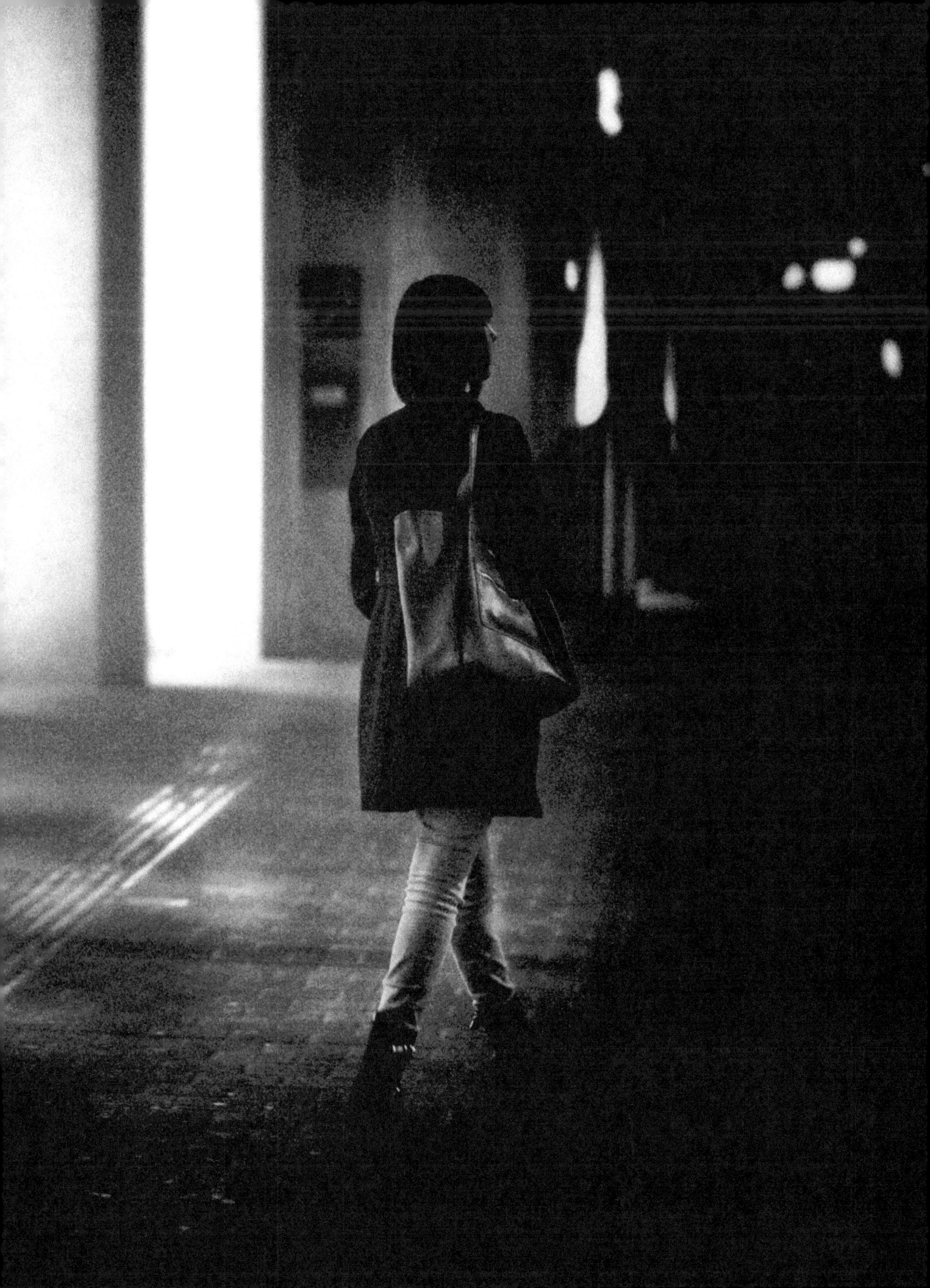

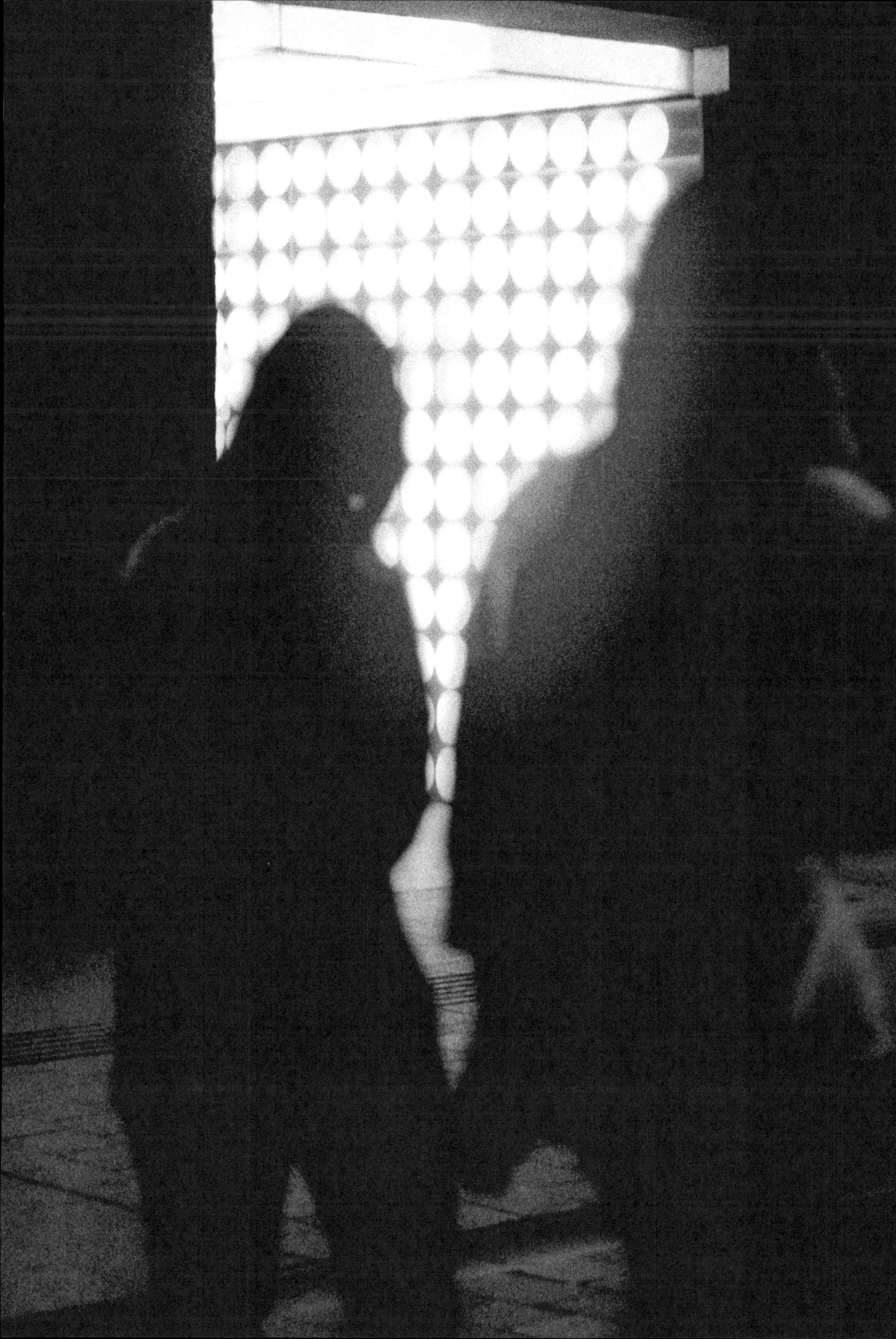

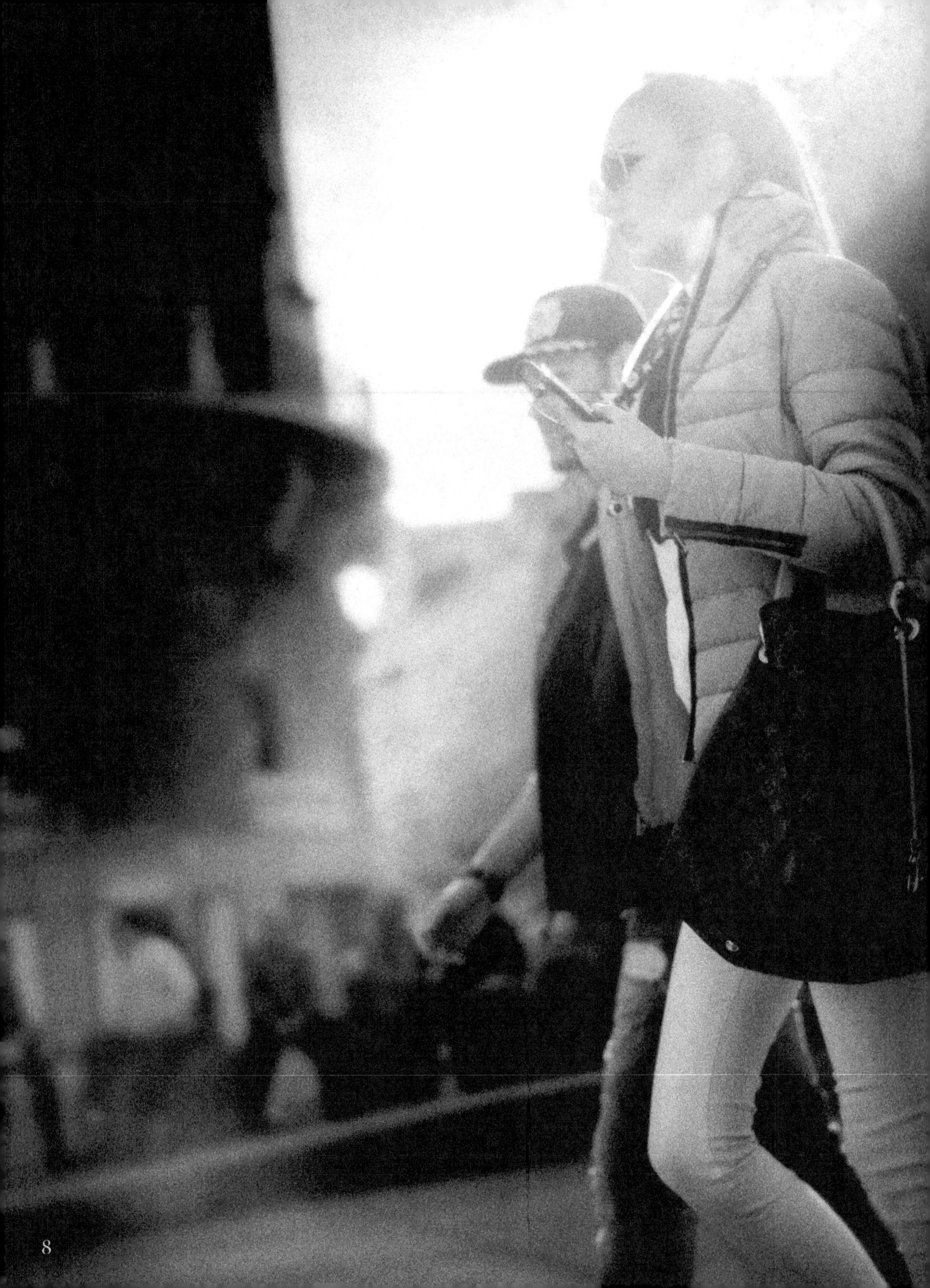

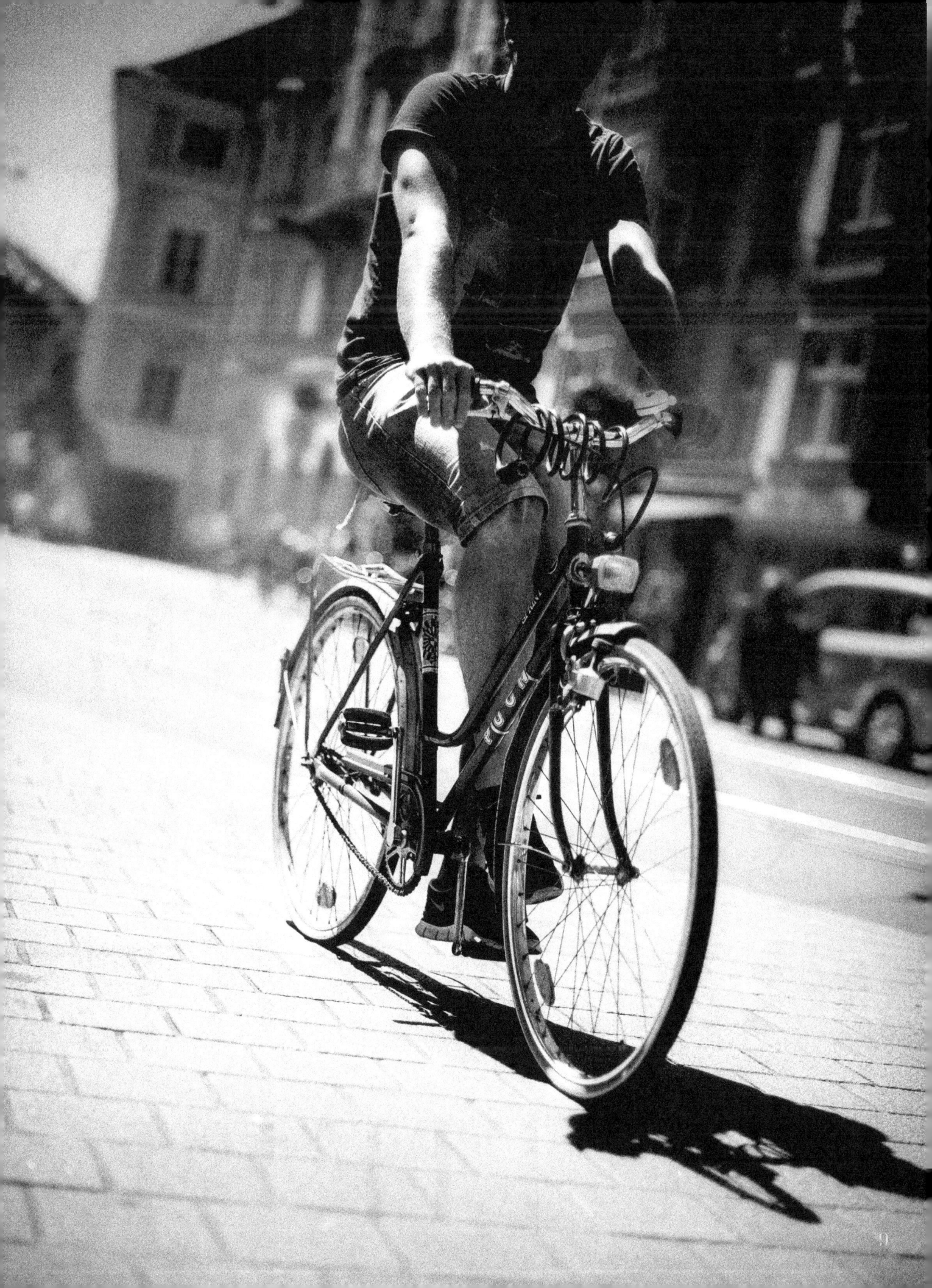

STYLEFASHIONSTREETBUSINESSMONEYMOMENTBEAUTIFUL

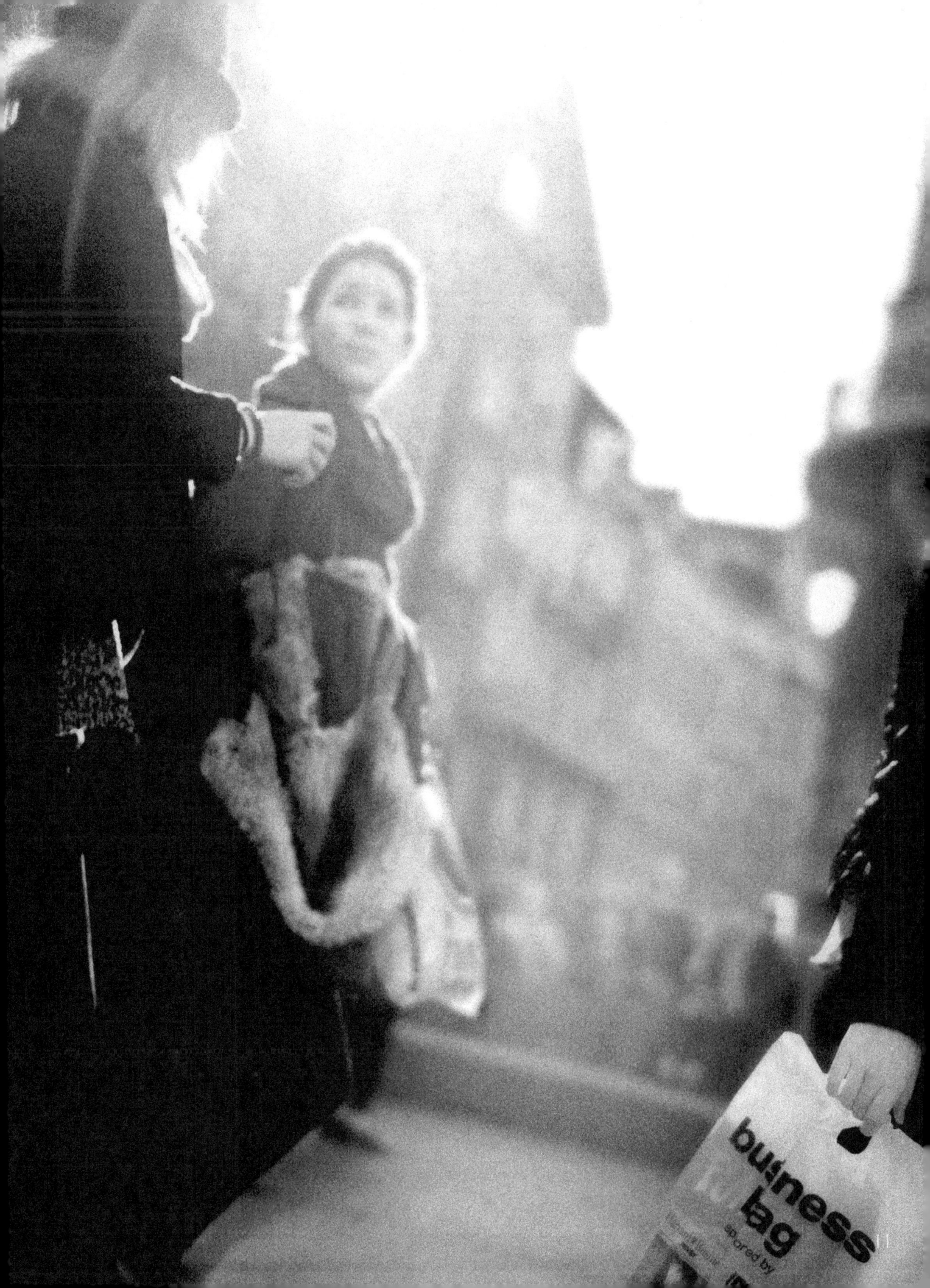

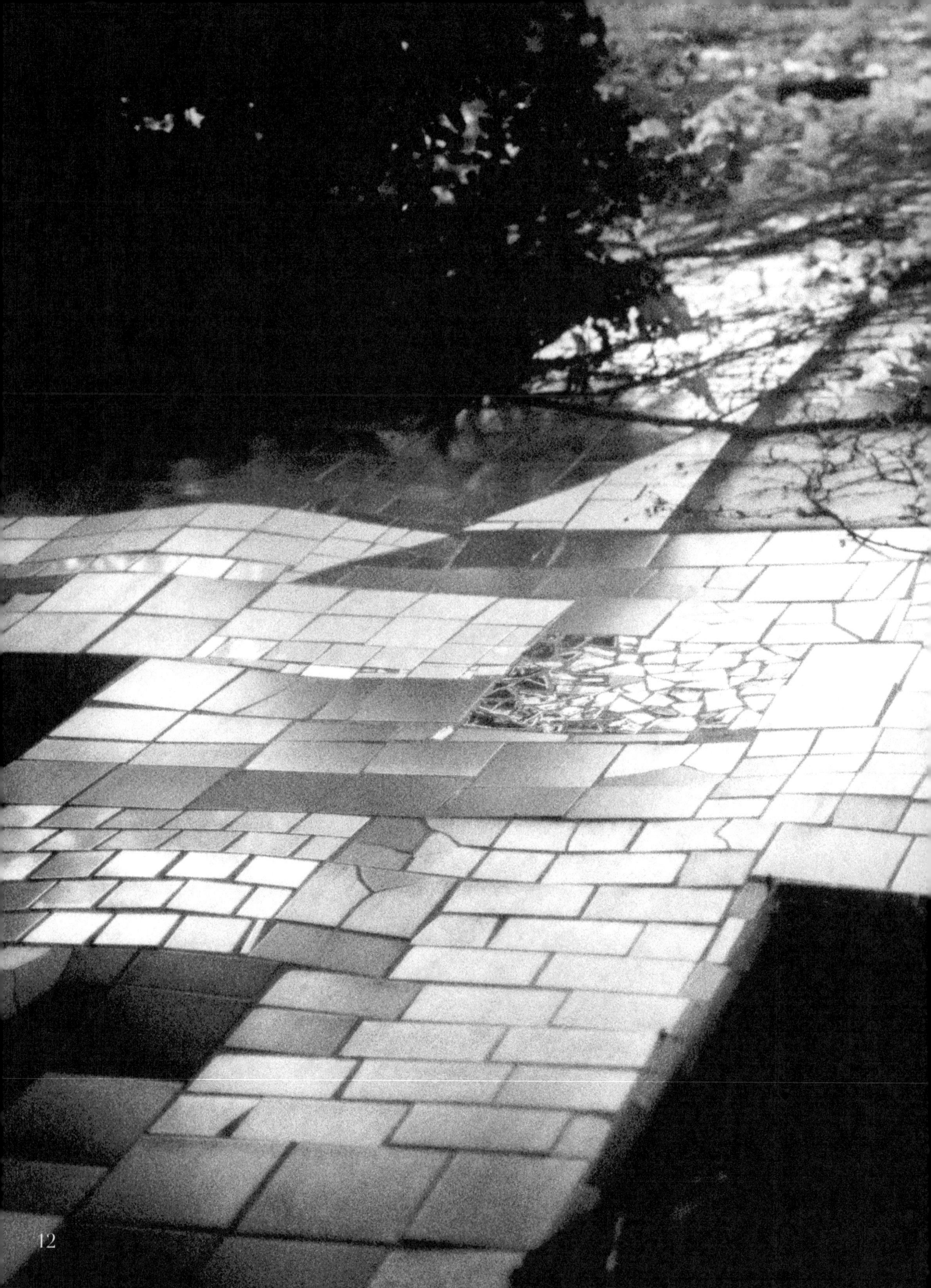

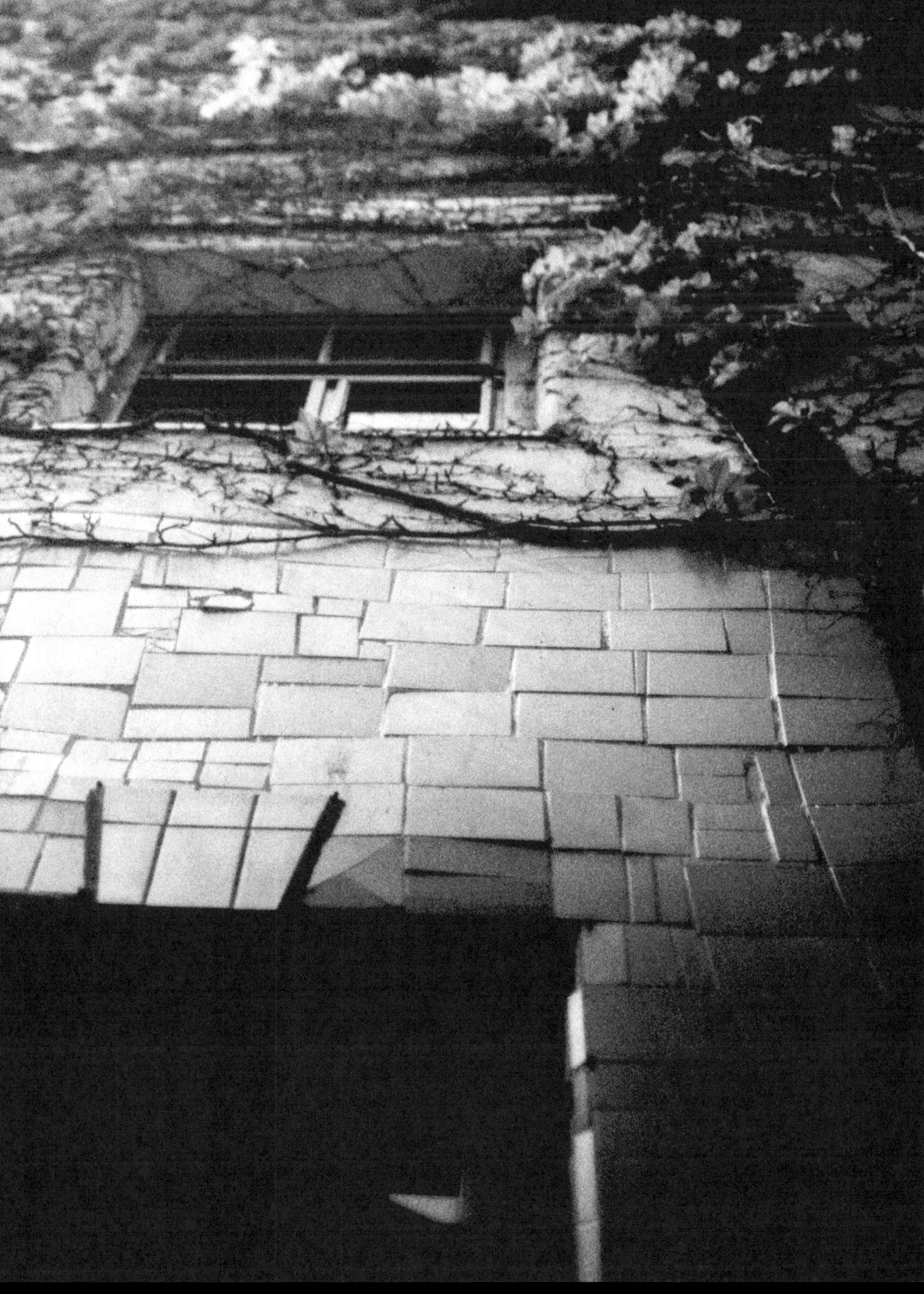

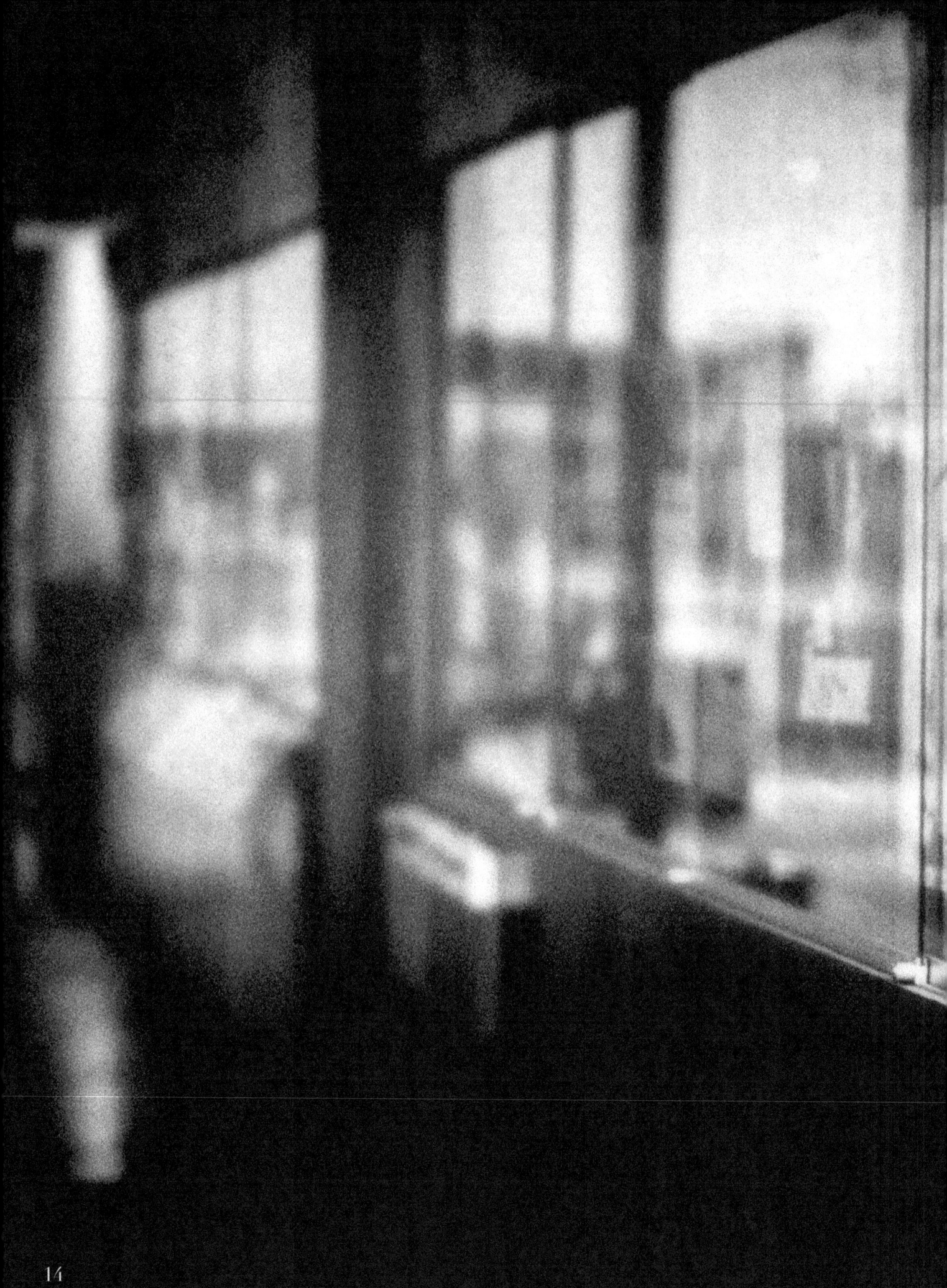

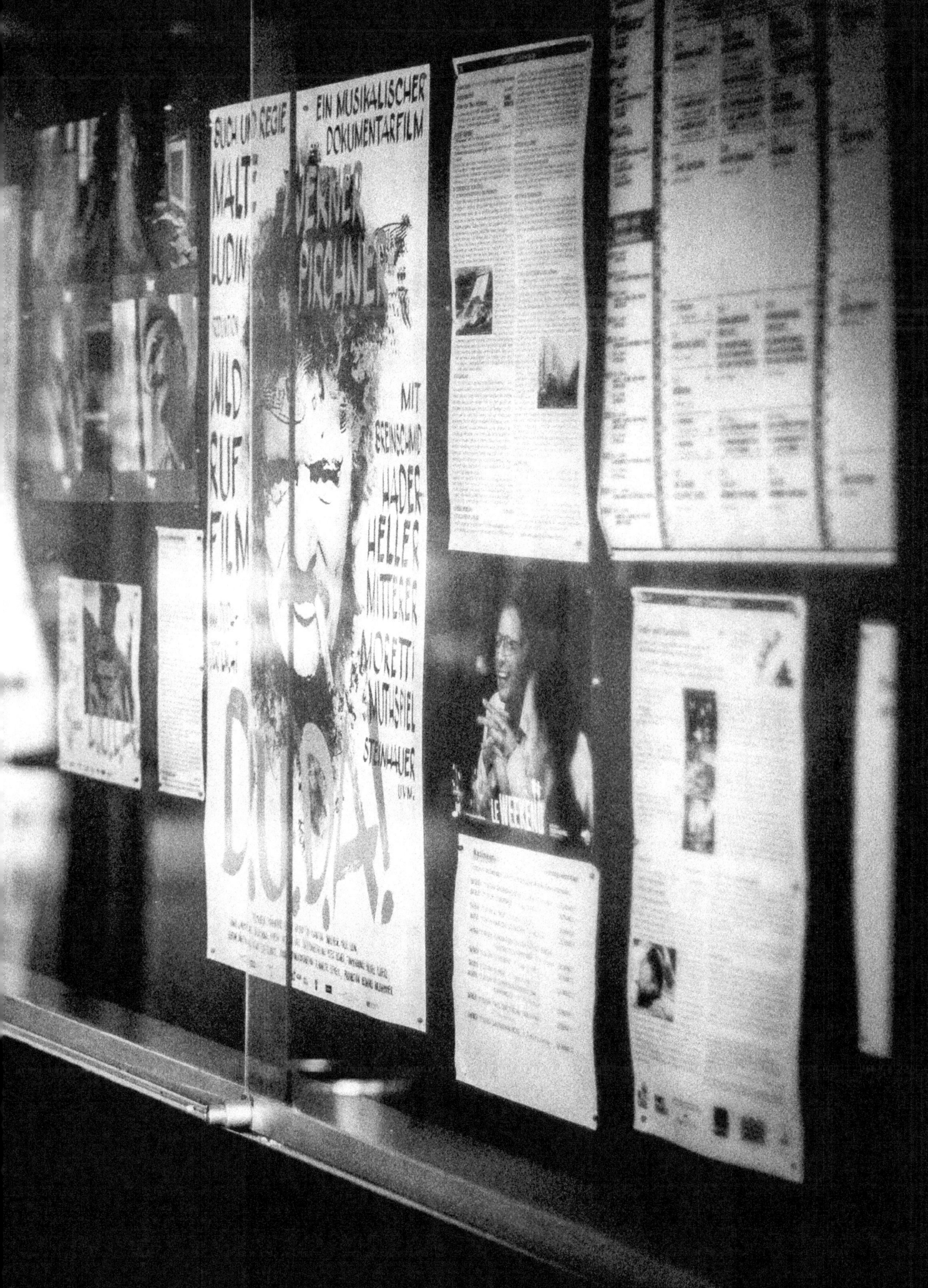

T R E N D G
R O O V E V
O G U E Y O
U N G O U
T F I T S C
L A S S Y

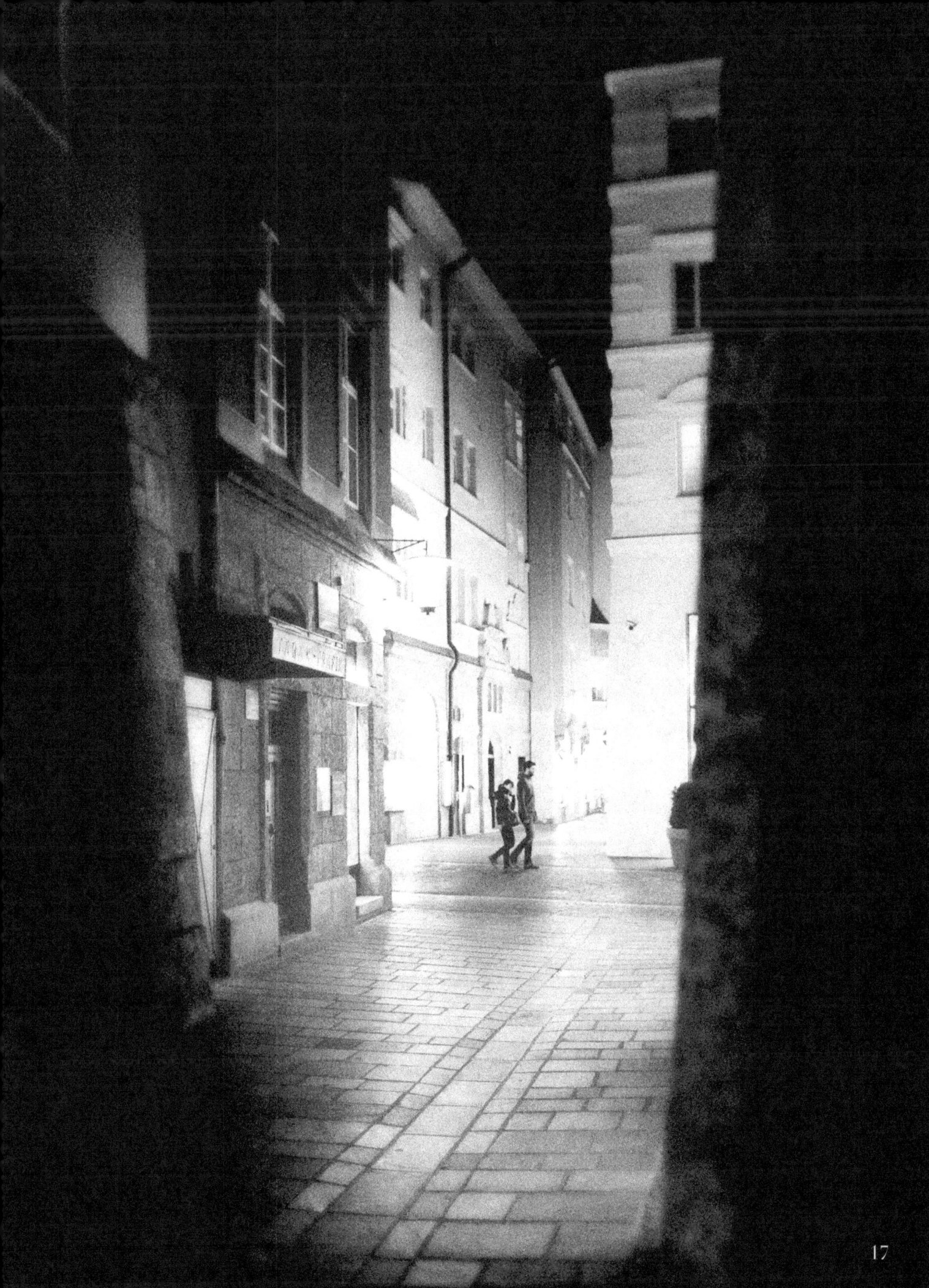

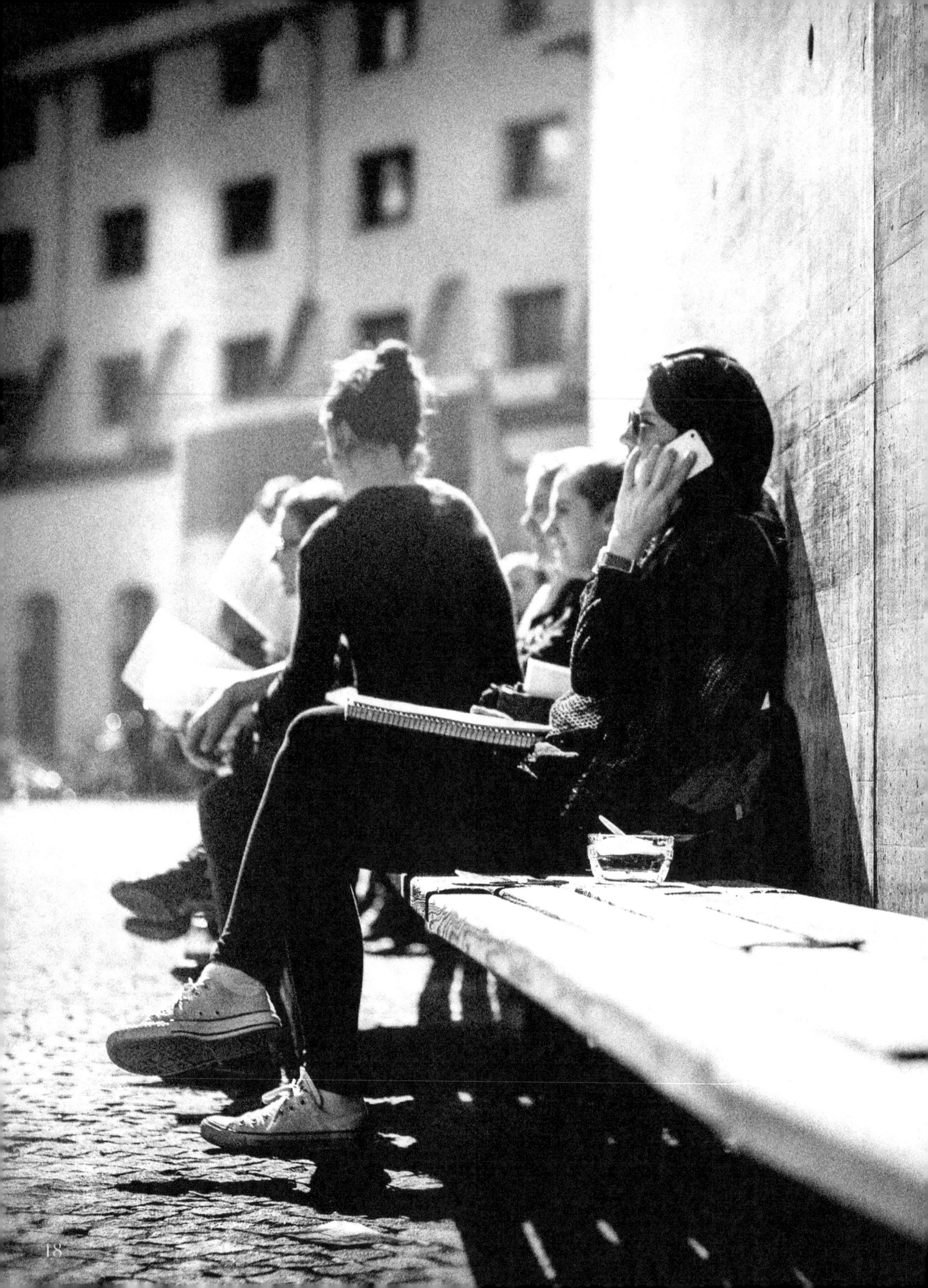

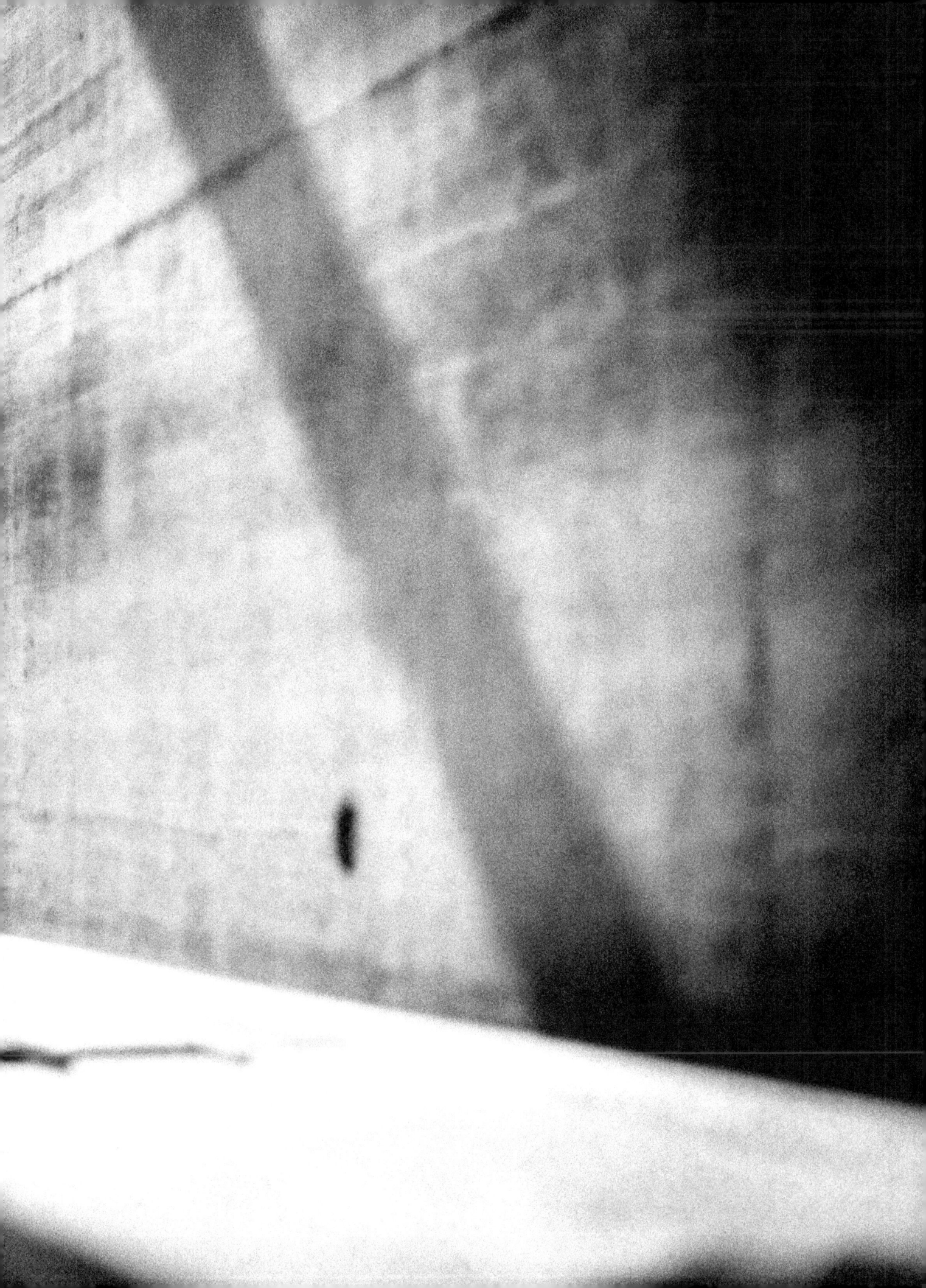

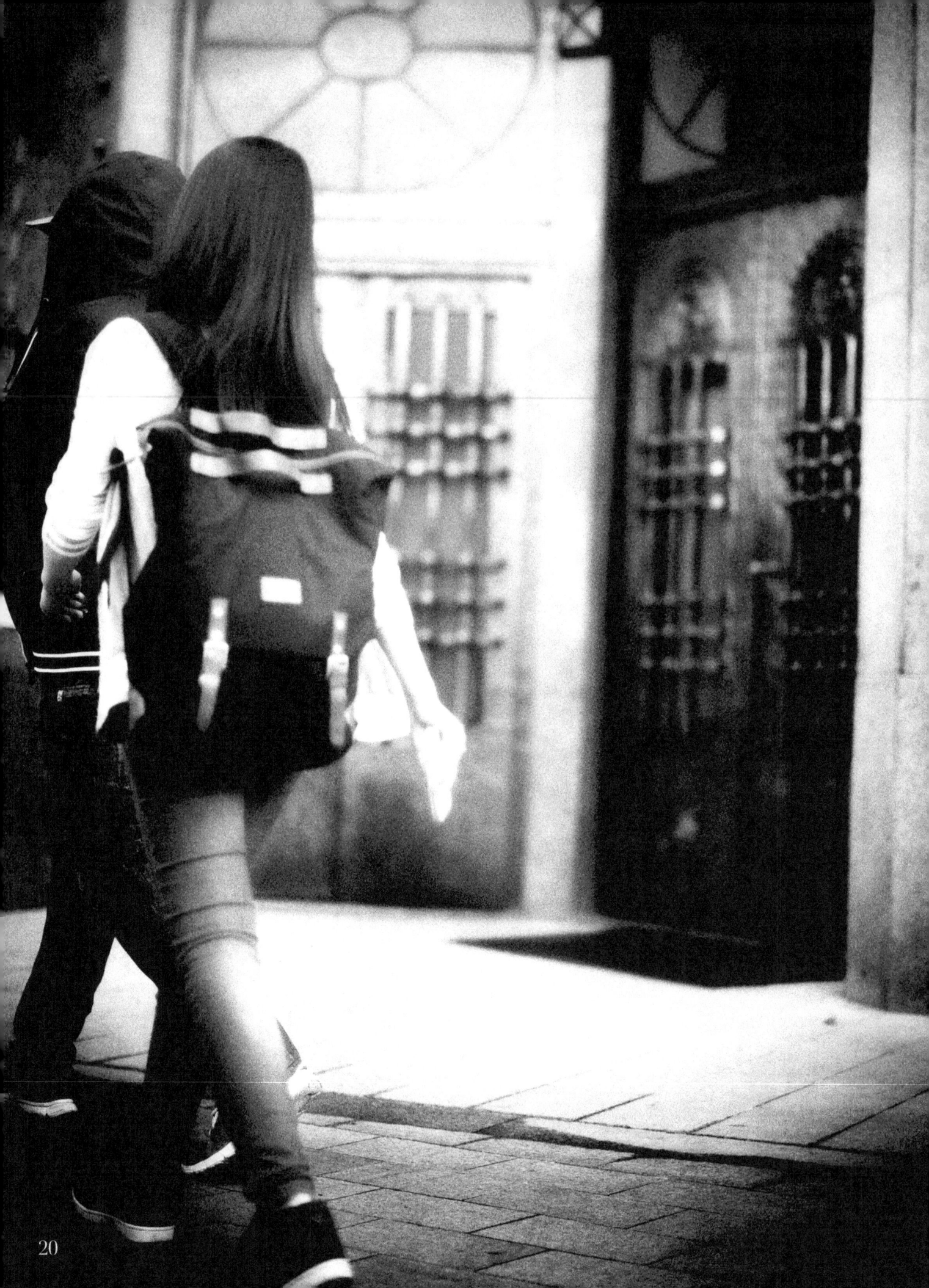

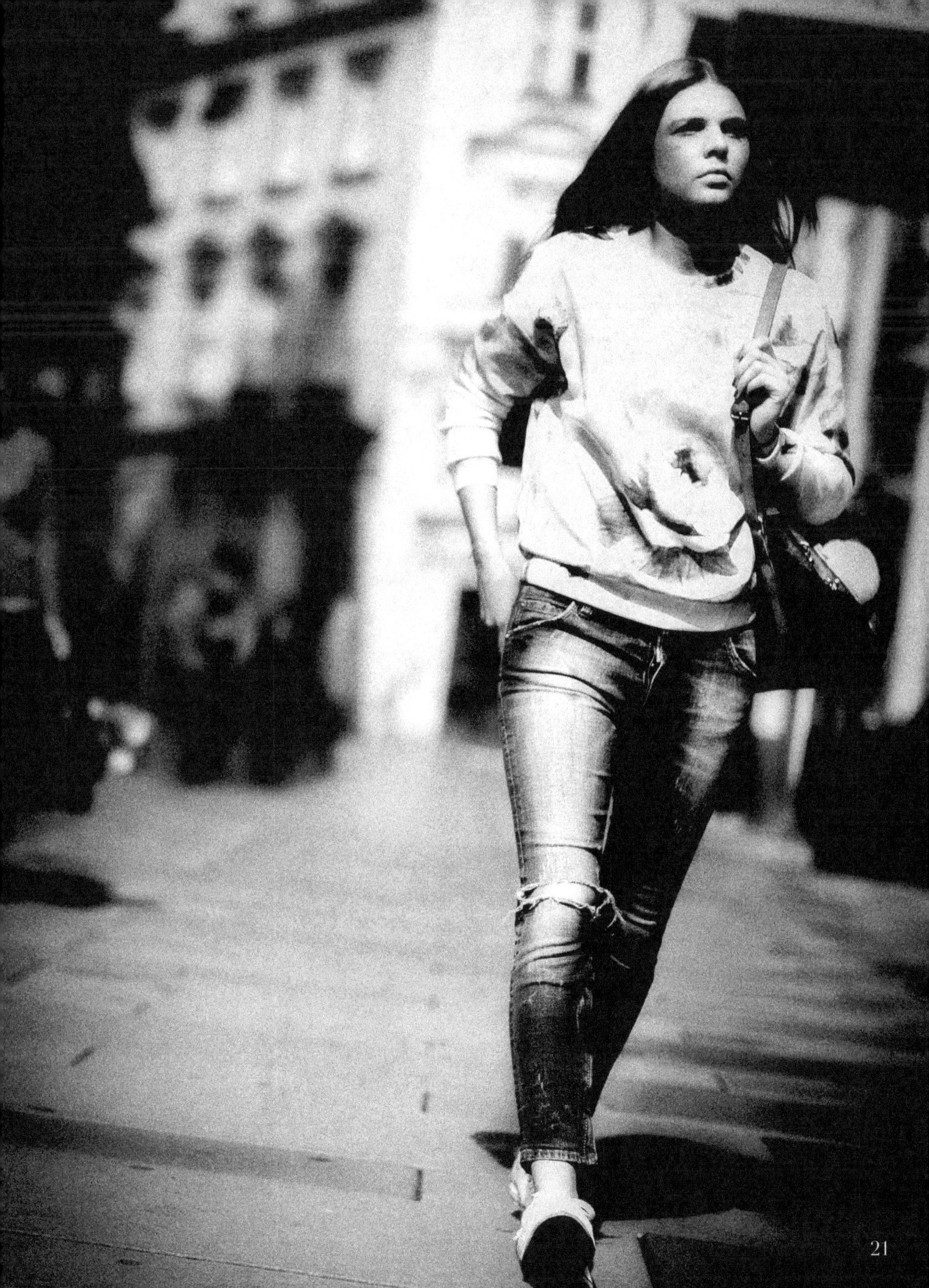

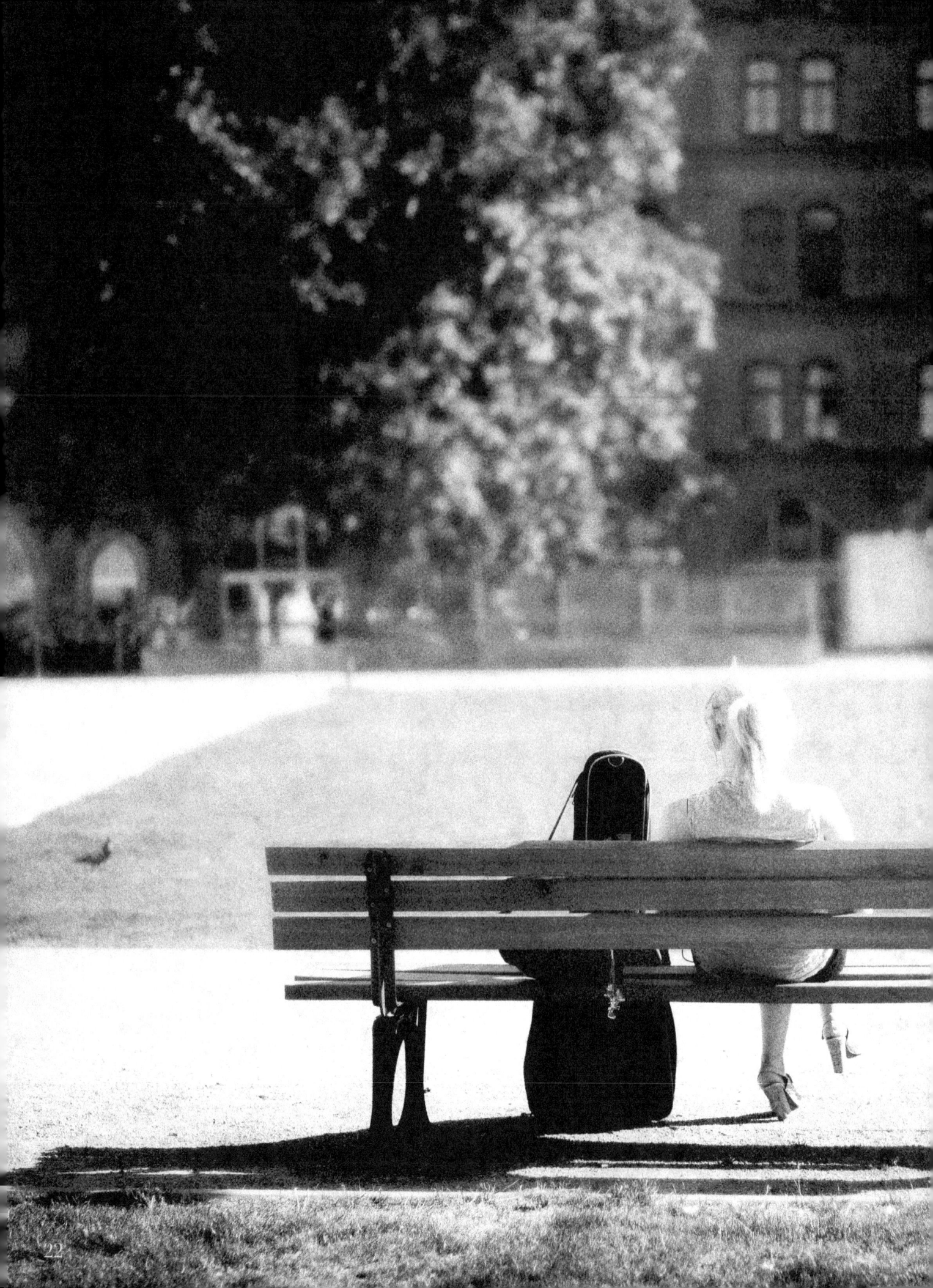

BOULEV
ARDEM
OTIONS
OULSPIRI
TMOVEM
ENTSOC
IALSHOW

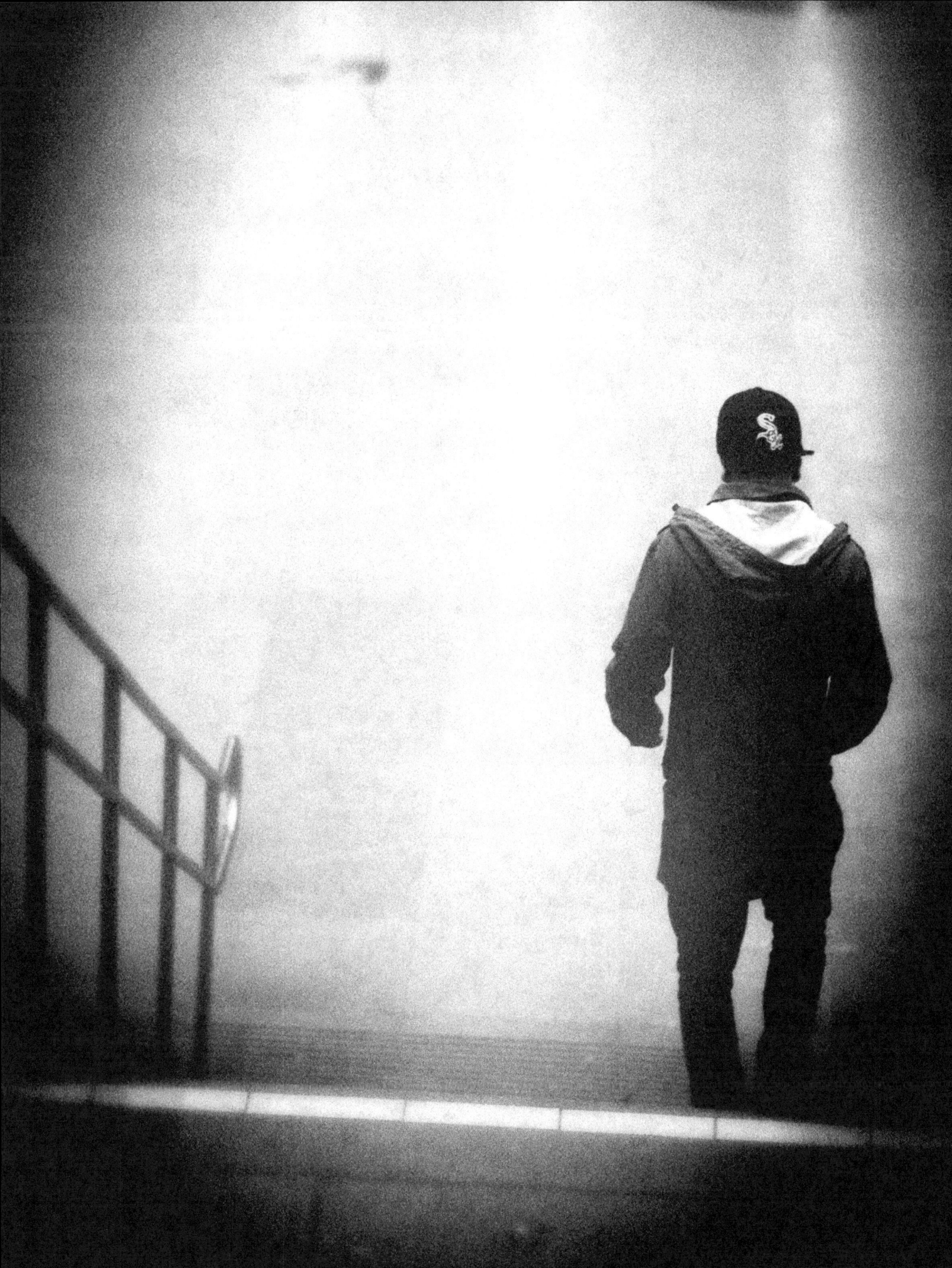

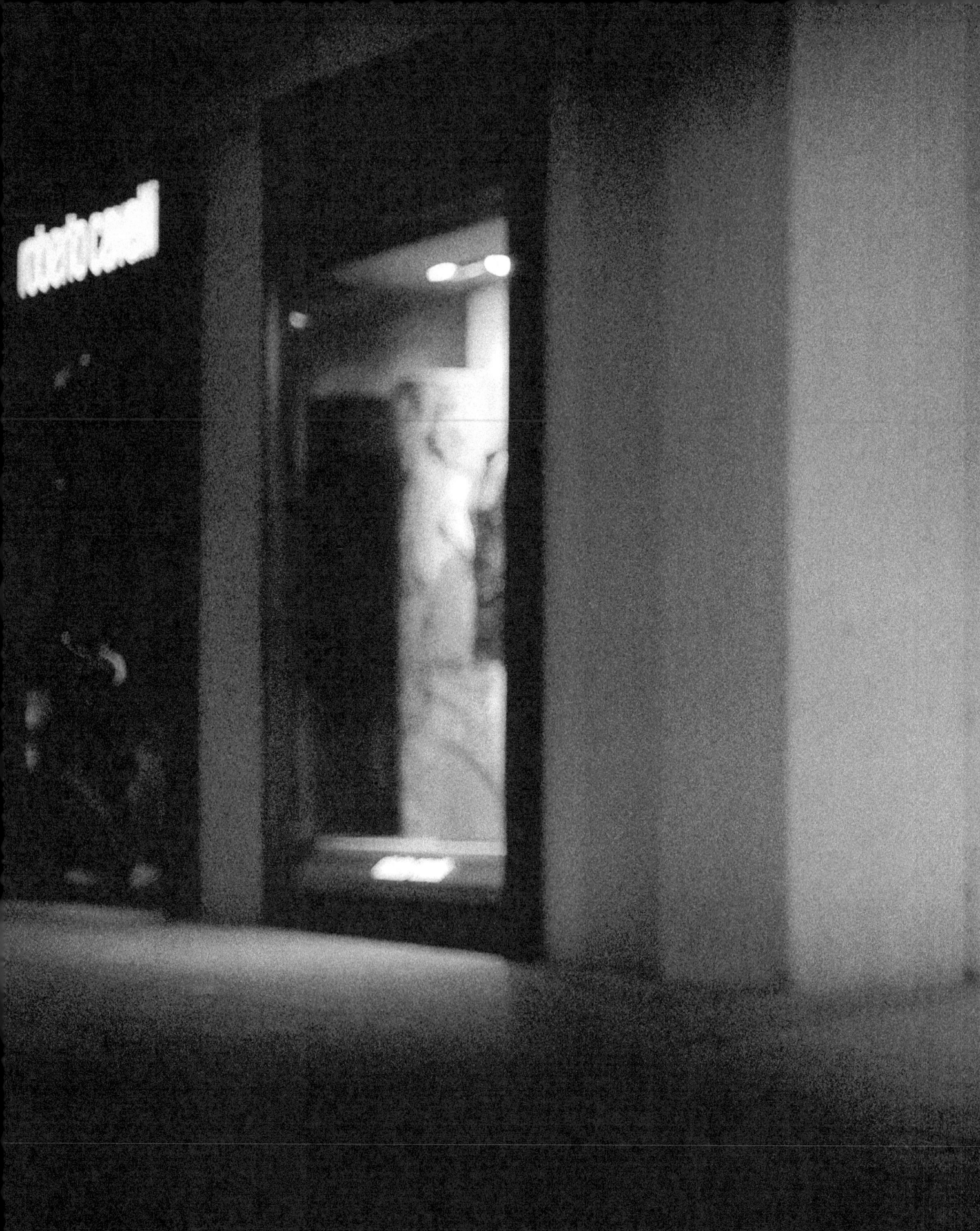

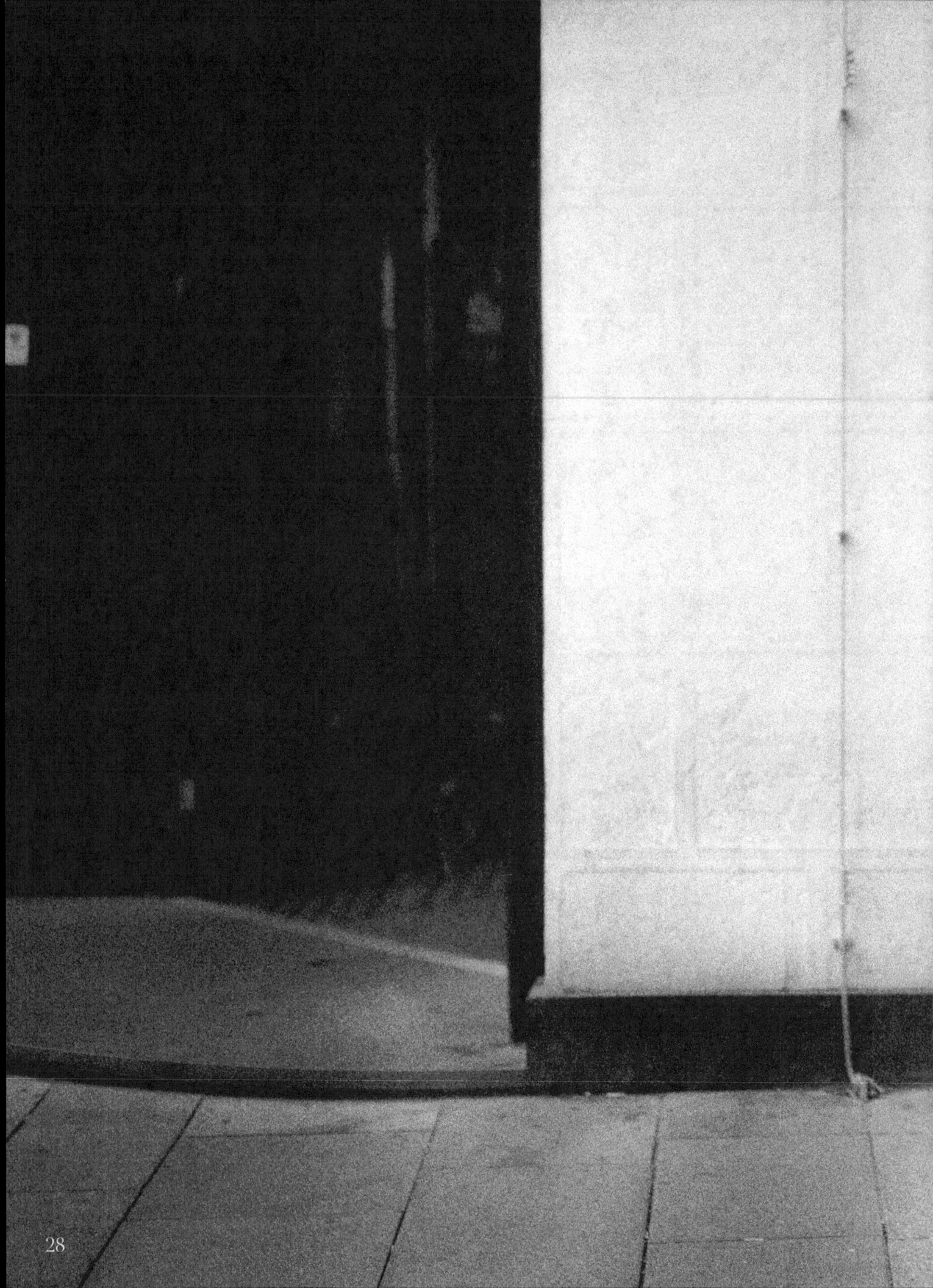

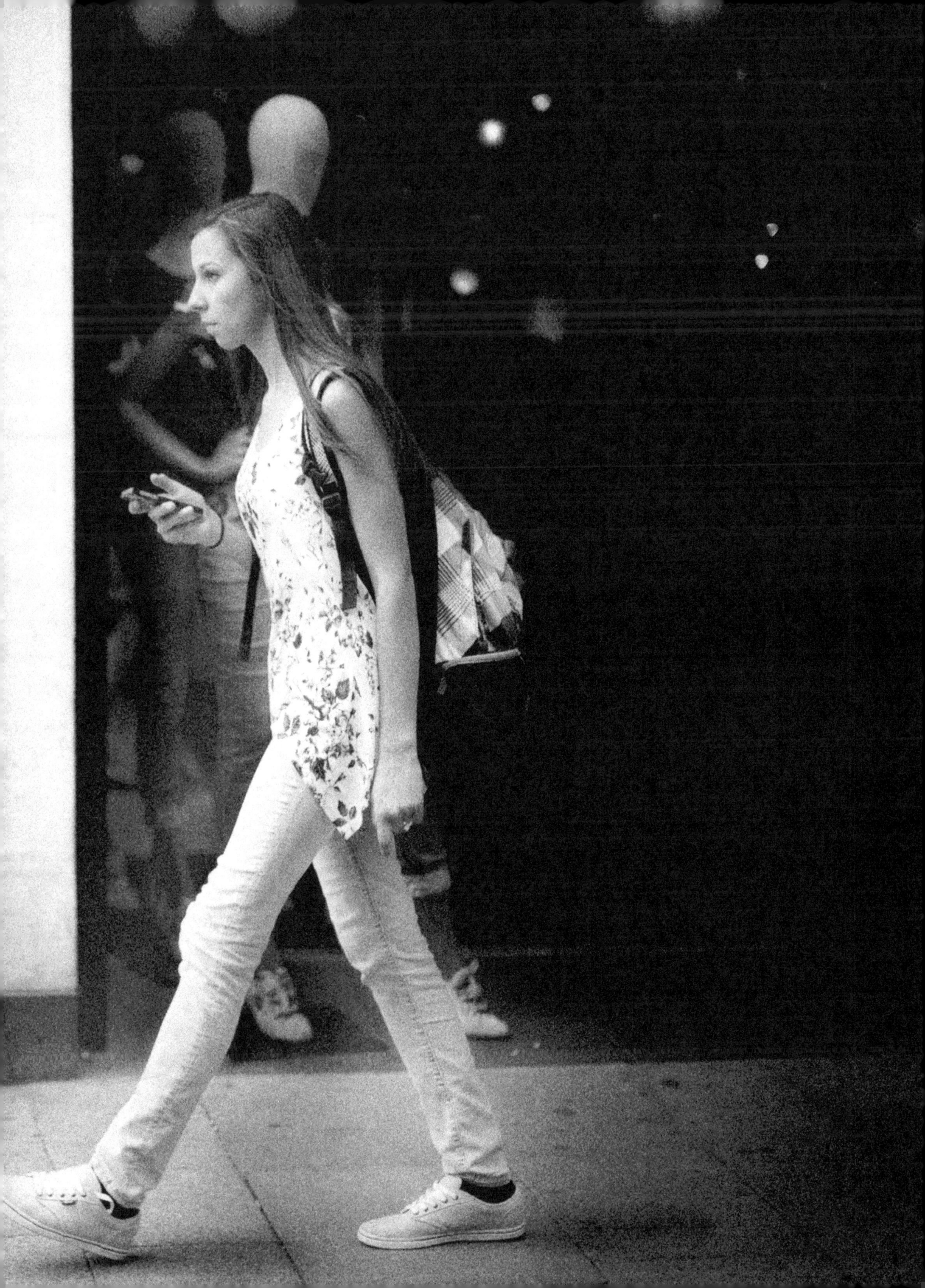

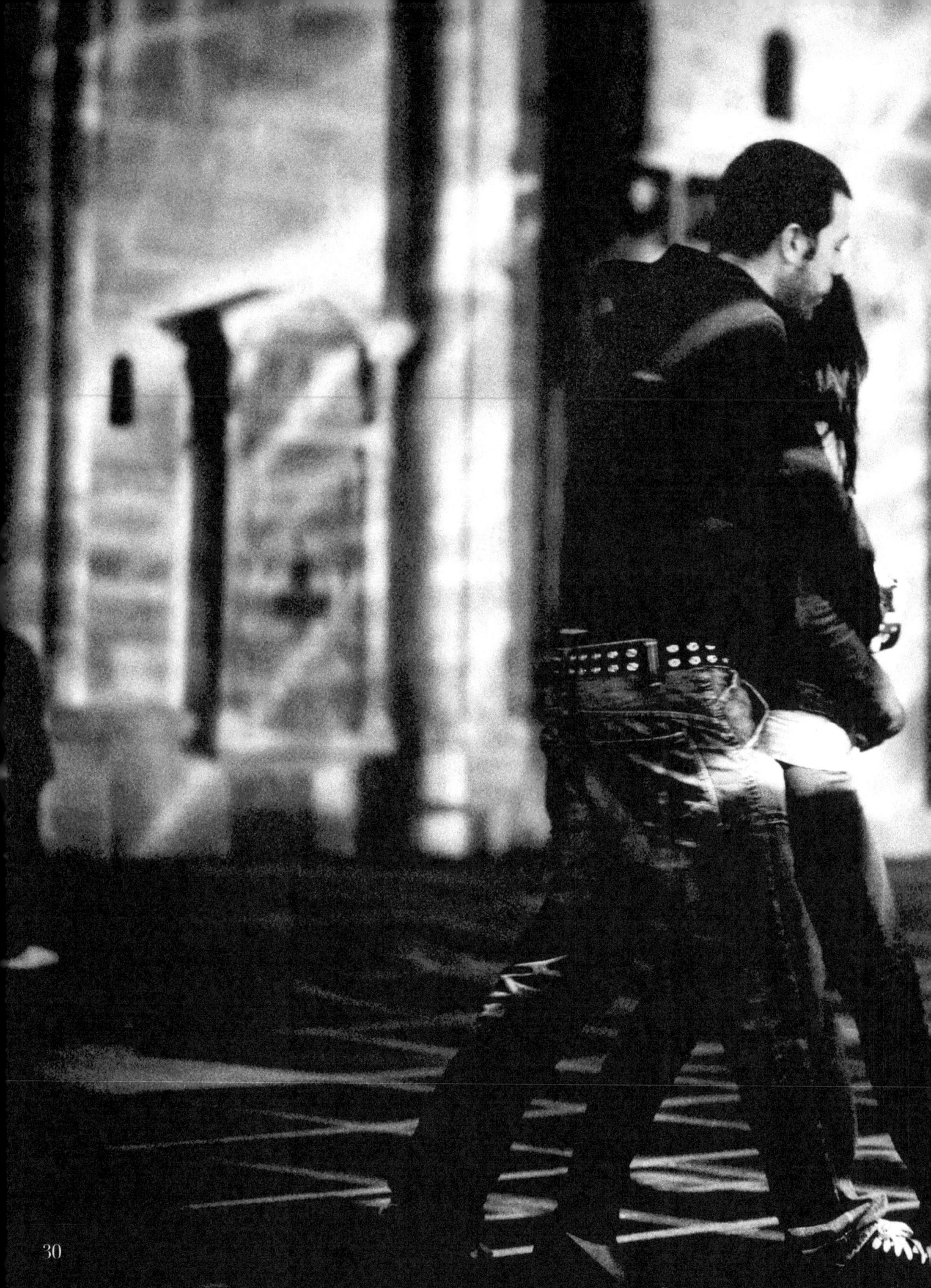

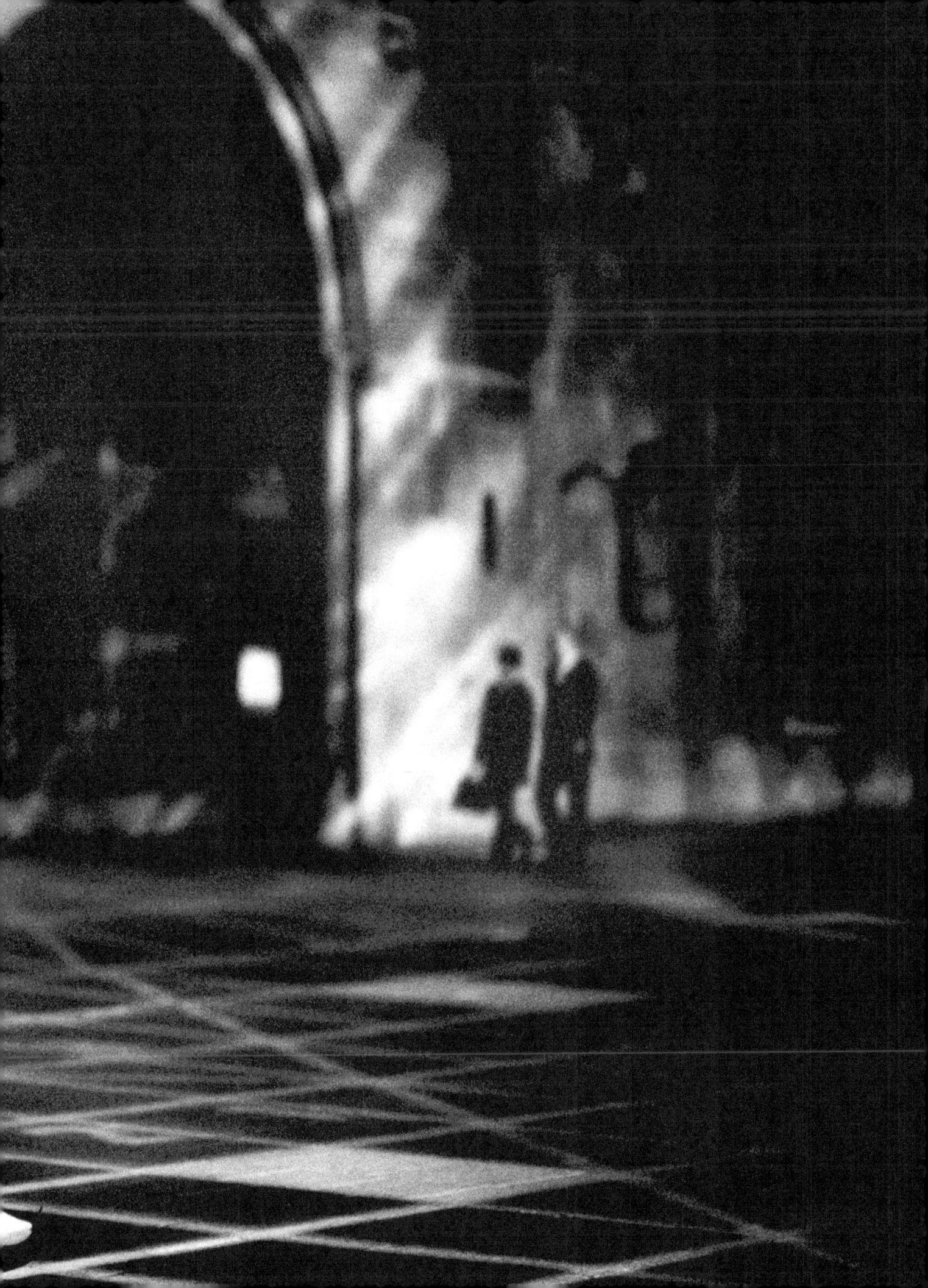

BRANDM
ARKETIN
GREVENU
EVOLUME
PROFITA
BILITYTU
RNOVER

INDEX

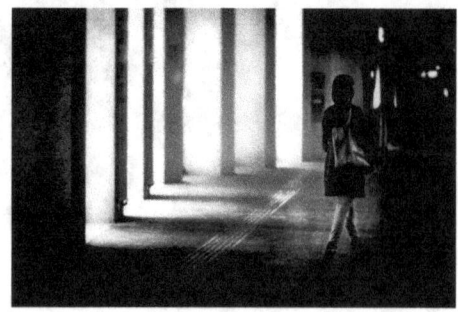
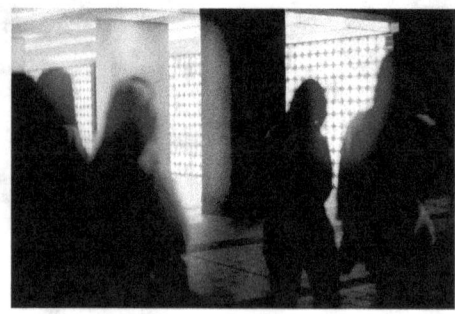
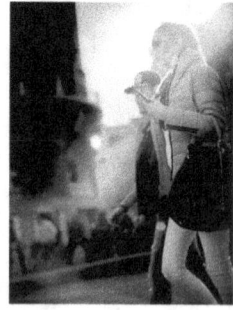
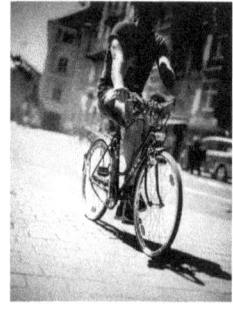
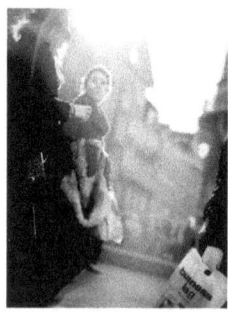
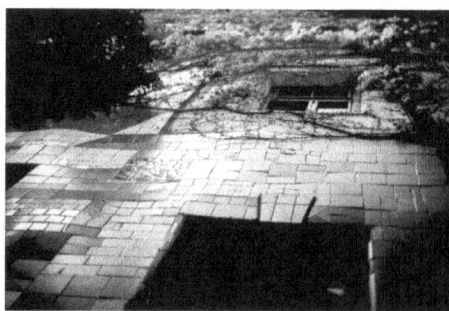
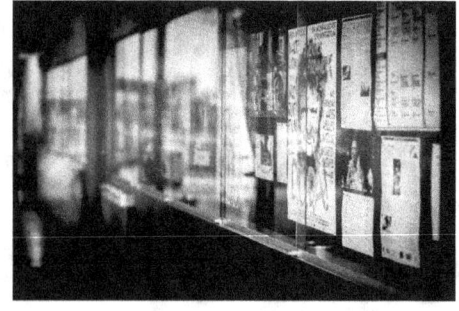
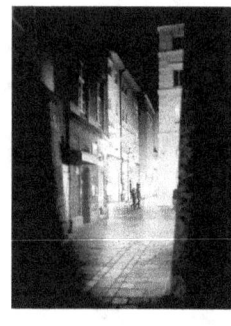
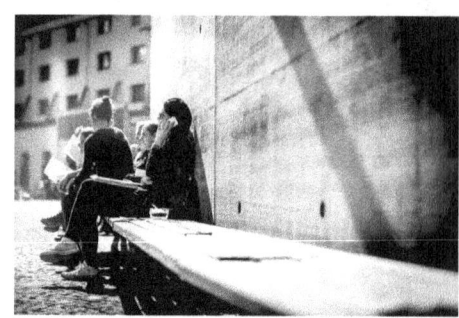

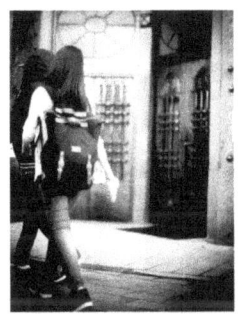

p20
Backpackers
2014

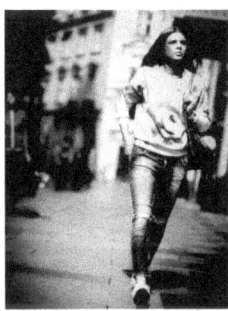

p21
Decisive girl
2014

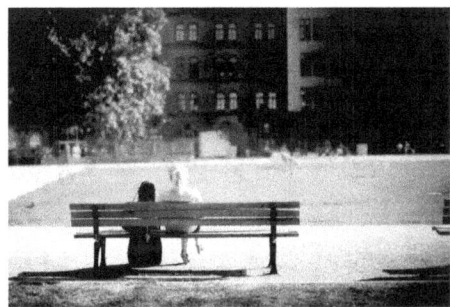

p22
Before the play
2014

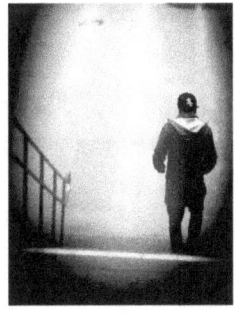

p25
Baseball cap
2014

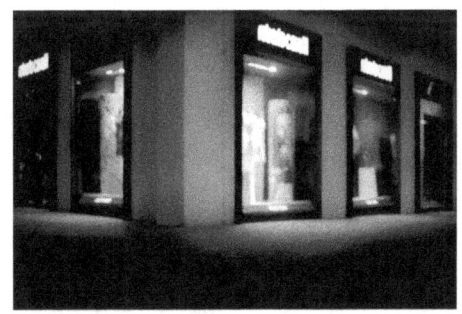

p26
Shopping break
2014

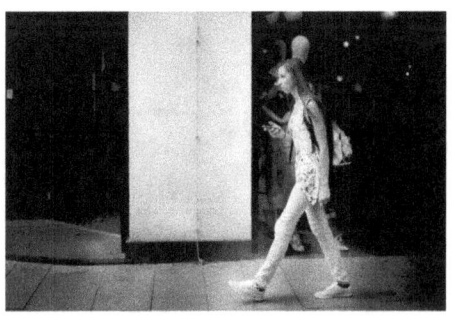

p28
Holding close
2014

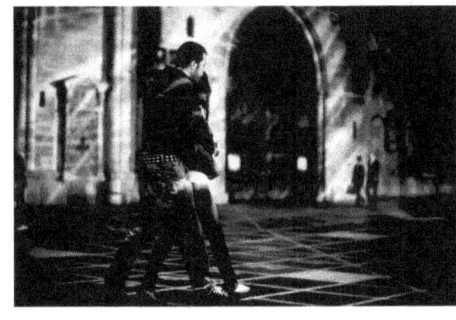

p30
Lovers strolling
2014

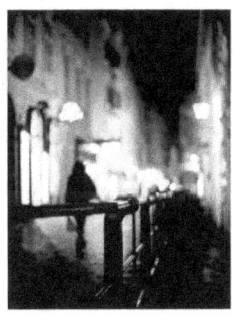

p33
Street lamps
2014

Acknowledgements

Roswitha & Peter Steiner for the genes and stuff

—

My friends for their support and motivation

—

My willing models for their patience

—

The Reddit photography community for getting the ball rolling

—

Nikon for their amazing gear

All persons in this book have been photographed in public spaces and solely as anonymous part of my artistic expression of the surrounding street scenery.

Josef-Pöll-Str. 19
6020 Innsbruck - Austria
www.photosteiner.com

Printed by Amazon
ISBN 978-1500434175

For image licensing or exhibition enquiries, please contact via email at office@photosteiner.com or telefax at +43 (0) 720 881900